Adam C. Laningham, M.Ed.,
Lin Lim, Ph.D.,
& Val Wilson, M.Ed.

What Parents Need To Know

Part of the Series:
Twice-Exceptional Children -
From Struggling to Thriving

A Bright Child Books, LLC Publication

For more information, contact:
adam@brightchildbooks.com

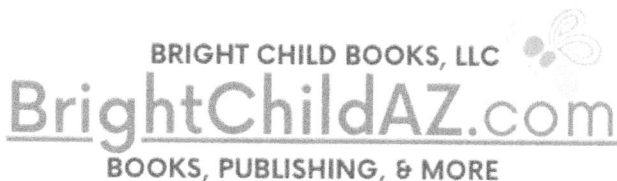

BRIGHT CHILD BOOKS, LLC

BrightChildAZ.com

BOOKS, PUBLISHING, & MORE

Edited by Gayle G. Bentley
Educational Consultant, The Bentley Center

Cover art by
Adam Laningham
Eye logo by M.Gibson

Contents

Acknowledgments

The authors would like to thank:

Our families for their support over the years.

All the many students we have worked with and who have taught us to be better educators.

Purpose

The purpose of this book is to help the adults of twice-exceptional children better understand and support them. The authors have extensive experience researching, educating, and parenting these children. We hope that whether you are parenting a child attending a brick-and-mortar school, an online school, or a homeschool, it is a valuable support to you and your child.

This is the first book of our series, Twice-Exceptional Children: From Struggling to Thriving. Our second book, available now is: What Educators Need to Know. Further books in the series, that are soon to be released, focus on educational strategies for the classroom, school administrators, and support for mental health professionals.

Introduction

Why We Wrote This Book

As lifelong educators, Val and Adam have worked with thousands of children and families over the years. Val has worked in multiple schools, teaching gifted children from various backgrounds and ages. Adam has taught in numerous schools and served as a district-level manager for gifted services in a large and diverse school district. Lin understands the parenting journey of complex outliers as a parent of a radically-accelerated, profoundly gifted daughter and a profoundly gifted and twice-exceptional (2e) son.

In addition, Lin is the Dean of Students and Communications at Bridges Graduate School of Cognitive Diversity in Education (BGS), with a Ph.D. in Human Development Psychology from Boston University, an Academic Graduate Certificate in Twice-exceptional Education from BGS, and an Academic Graduate Certificate in Mind, Brain, and Education from Johns Hopkins University.

Fortunately, most children do just fine in our schools and become successful adults. That said, we know many children struggle in our educational system. If you are a parent of a struggling child, you know it can be heartbreaking for children and their families.

Many reasons result in students not thriving in school. Every child and person is an individual. Some children have learning disabilities, while others have complicated home lives. Some students struggle socially, and some have unique sensory, emotional, or physical needs. This book was written for parents with children having difficulty in school because of their unique learning needs due to dynamic interactions between discrepancies in areas of high and low (absolute or relative) abilities. (*In other words, their children are very bright in some areas but struggle in others.*) Though the number of students **formally identified educationally** to fit into this category makes up a small percentage of our population, finding ways to support them is quite challenging. In addition, some would also argue that many children unofficially fit into this category.

This book is meant to explain the complexities of 2e children in accessible ways and provide strategies to support them in their learning journey. We hope this also empowers parents to use the contents in this book to increase public awareness and understanding of 2e children. Raising a child takes a whole community, and you are not alone.

This book will provide strategies that help the adults support the children in their lives. It is meant to be a practical, easy-to-access resource for parents, as well as educators, based on the research and strategies three veteran gifted educators have used to support all kinds of children, including twice-exceptional, over their careers.

This book is written from a collaboration of researchers, educators, and parental voices so parents understand what happens in the classroom. This understanding empowers parents to make informed, intentional choices to support gifted and struggling children holistically.

Book Study & Reflection Questions

Each chapter includes pages with questions to help the reader think about important concepts. The questions are meant to springboard the reader into a better understanding as they reflect on the content and can also serve as discussion starters for book studies or groups. Space is intentionally left open for you to take notes and jot down your thoughts.

Let's get started...

C's voice,

"Hard things are easy, easy things are hard!"

"Why say "can you"… when I have no choice in the answer?"

"Why not?"   "Why am I different?"

*"I don't know how I got the answer;
I just know·"*

"What if...."   *"Actually...."*

"I feel our insignificance."
(human beings within the vast universe)

"Why do people ask how are you when they are not interested in the answer?"

"Which eye do you want me to look at?"

"Too busy thinking."   "Data is beautiful and calming."

"NO WORDS TO DESCRIBE MY FEELINGS."

Check out "C for Curiosity," a photo journey of our world through the eyes of C, a neurodiverse multicultural twice-exceptional child at: https://youtu.be/XlI3wNaxrP0 (selective narration by C)

A Chapter of Lin's Journey Through 2e

My family first encountered the term "twice-exceptional" when our son C was given a psycho-educational assessment in second grade. The discrepancies between and within subsections of the IQ and achievement assessments provided quantitative data that reinforced my parental instincts that something was happening with my son that we had yet to understand.

C is a highly verbal, social, curious boy who began playing the violin at two and a half years old. He composed a violin-piano duet at seven years old. It was titled "Fly in Amber" and described a beautiful yet sorrowful depiction of a fly trapped in amber and turned into a valuable object after its death.

His development resembles a staircase, from single words to whole sentences, sitting to walking, silent "reading" to reading entire sentences aloud, smiling to screaming. He is the child who can instantly tell you the speed of a baseball thrown from one moving car to another moving in the opposite direction but cannot explain how he "just knows." Yet, he has a difficult time retrieving his multiplication facts. **He seems to be multiple ages all at once.**

He is also a child with significant challenges with handwriting, producing written output, tying his shoelaces, and managing multiple sensory sensitivities. C functions like a light switch - either "on" or "off," and nothing in between. C presented through fifth grade as a "bright but..." type of child (with his giftedness compensating for his disability) within our public school. Over time, a child similar to C may start performing educationally as a "normal" child, then a "non-gifted special education" child. This tendency toward an educational presentation of disability overshadowing gifts over time occurs when high and low abilities are not recognized and understood as interacting dynamically. High- and low-ability needs must be considered simultaneously to address curricular needs appropriately.

What happens when we lead with strengths *and* consider how low abilities get in the way of successfully completing learning goals? Does C need to show content mastery of lesson units only through handwriting when he is dysgraphic?

Below is a sample of C's writing when he was eight years old.

Gramar Bootcamp 9/27/16

Oreo is our class pet.
Scholars work thier best.

Every day the scholars drive
mrs. Austin nutty!

The noisy students tak to
much!

A juicy apple fell down
the tree.

Here is C's essay output from when he was provided with a scribe at eight years old.

My favorite time of year will be in December of 2020 when Saturn aligns with Jupiter because it is a rare occurence and I would love to see the sky.

This phenomenon is so rare that it only happens once every 18-20 years. The last time these two celestial bodies crossed paths was in 2000. That was eight years before I was born. When it happens again, I will be 12!

I am most excited to see this alignment because I have heard the sky looks creepy, like somebody turned on a light bulb. I don't know for sure because I haven't seen it, but I imagine that the two planets will look like a donut. The ring is Saturn's rings, the middle of the donut is Saturn, and a donut hole is Jupiter. I wonder what

Saturn's rings will taste like - chocolate or glazed!

I can't wait until December 2020 when I will see this rare event. The sky will look so weird. So, what will Saturn's rings taste like? You don't know? Don't skimp on the details: chocolate or glazed?!

C's handwriting at 13 years old

C is a child where handwriting will always be very challenging. So, what is a parent to do? What did we do?

In our case, technology saved C's life. He was supported with explicit instructions and opportunities to learn how to type first. After he was sufficiently proficient in learning to type, this task was scaffolded to apply typing to complete classwork.

We also tried using speech-to-text and encouraged him to draw his thoughts in response to the writing assignments as a prewriting organizational tool. Although speech-to-text seemed to work well for C, his self-awareness of using speech-to-text in the classroom made him concerned about making him too "different" from his classmates. This meant that for C's social-emotional health, speech-to-text within the classroom was not a good fit.

In contrast, drawing out his thoughts in response to a writing assignment in the classroom seemed to help provide a positive scaffold to organize C's thoughts better before he started typing out the answers.

In a nutshell, experiment with your child collaboratively, and listen to their feedback. Some things work better in different contexts (home versus school, alone versus in a group), and they are also subject to changes over time as your child's body, mind, and brain mature over time.

Introduction

Book Study & Reflection Questions

Reflect on Lin's experience with her son. Have you had a similar situation with your child? What stood out in your mind?

What are some areas of strength you have?

What are some areas you feel like you are more
challenged in?

How do you cope with your areas of weakness and enjoy your areas of strength?

How about your son or daughter? How do they cope with their areas of weakness and enjoy their areas of strength?

Chapter 1
Who Are We?

Children and individuals are all unique. Yet, despite our understanding of human uniqueness, we often need to group or categorize ourselves and others into groups for various reasons. We then assign different attributes and characteristics to those in these groups. The education field is no different.

The problem is that not everyone in that group shares the assigned traits, and we also have individuals who fit into multiple groups. This is certainly the case with twice-exceptional (2e) children.

Sally Reis, Susan Baum, and Edith Burke published a commonly cited operational definition of 2e learners. The definition resulted from a National Commission on Twice-Exceptional Students deliberations with different stakeholder input, including researchers, universities, K-12 schools, psychologists, educational therapists, national and state association presidents, and graduate students.

Their definition is as follows:

Twice-exceptional learners are students who demonstrate the potential for high achievement or creative productivity in one or more domains such as math, science, technology, the social arts, the visual, spatial, or performing arts, or other areas of human productivity AND who manifest one or more disabilities as defined by federal or state eligibility criteria.

These disabilities include specific learning disabilities; speech and language disorders; emotional/behavioral disorders; physical disabilities; Autism Spectrum Disorders (ASD); or other health impairments, such as Attention Deficit/Hyperactivity Disorder (ADHD). These disabilities and high abilities combine to produce a unique population of students who may fail to demonstrate either high academic performance or specific disabilities. Their gifts may mask their disabilities, and their disabilities may mask their gifts.

Identification of twice-exceptional students requires comprehensive assessment in both the areas of giftedness and disabilities, as one does not preclude the other. Identification, when possible, should be conducted by professionals from both disciplines and, when possible, by those with knowledge about twice exceptionality to address the impact of co-incidence/co-morbidity of both areas on diagnostic assessments and eligibility requirements for services.

Educational services must identify and serve both the high achievement potential and the academic and social-emotional deficits of this population of students. Twice-exceptional students require differentiated instruction, curricular and instructional accommodations and/or modifications, direct services, specialized instruction, acceleration options, and opportunities for talent development that incorporate the effects of their dual diagnosis.

Twice-exceptional students require an individual education plan (IEP) or a 504 accommodation plan with goals and strategies that enable them to achieve at a level and rate commensurate with their abilities. This comprehensive education plan must include talent development goals, as well as compensation skills and strategies to address their disabilities and their social and emotional needs.

In summary -

The term 2e is a label created to classify individuals who are both gifted and have special learning needs. In other words, these children have an academic gift in one or more areas but also have a disability in one or more areas. Such children *learn differently* due to the interactions between their areas of high and low ability(s).

Being in just one of these groups (either gifted or special needs) can be very challenging for any child. For example, a child who is identified as gifted may have to overcome the expectations placed on them by having this term used for their abilities. Does being gifted mean you should be earning good grades? This is still a prevalent myth. Also, gifted children are often gifted in a particular area, yet overly high expectations may be placed on them in multiple academic areas. Truly understanding giftedness is still an area that we are working on to try to help both parents and educators understand what it is.

A student with a disability must also overcome those disabilities and any stigmas, labels, or expectations placed on them. Each label comes with certain <u>assumptions</u>, challenges, and judgments. Working through this can be challenging for any child.

Complexities of being twice-exceptional

Susan Baum, a pioneer in 2e understanding and teaching strategies, came across many bright children in special education, and it became her passion to find ways to nurture and understand such children for success. She used color metaphors* to help others better understand the complexities of 2e learners.

2e learners are always green, a color that emerges when you mix yellow (high ability) and blue (low/disability). "It is not easy being green," she likes to say to our graduate school students.

Building on Susan's work, we created our logo on the cover of this book. We hope the colors combined into the eye help to illustrate that we are learning to see the whole 2e child.

We believe you cannot address or truly see the 2e child without addressing both colors. Once we see the whole child, we need to support them by leading with their areas of strength.

*To read more about the work of Susan Baum and view a color visual, visit: www.2ecenter.org/definitions-and-resources/

Lin has since built upon Susan Baum's work to synthesize her 2e color metaphor through the lens of the N.E.S.T! perspective*, which is informed theoretically by dynamic systems as a contemporary approach to understanding 2e individuals' human development across time. In other words, who we are at any point in time is always the composite of interactions between our inner and outer worlds.

The N.E.S.T! perspective offers a paradigm shift and advocates for always **leading with your child's strengths** while considering how disabilities interact with successfully accomplishing each learning goal. This concept is very important, so we wanted to include the overview here. We have more resources that delve into this concept, as listed in the back of the book. This echoes Dr. Ross Greene's starting point that all children do well if they can. Therefore, when children struggle, we should view it as an indication that something is preventing them from reaching their potential.

More about the N.E.S.T! perspective and Lin's academic work can be found online at: zenliving.com

What are some general characteristics of twice-exceptional children?

Our friends at the Gifted Development Center developed a checklist* for recognizing common characteristics of 2e children.

This checklist is used as a screener to determine if formal assessments might be helpful. Assessments by professionals, well-trained in understanding 2e complexities, form important support teams for families.

We have summarized some of the general characteristics of 2e learners taken from their checklist on the following page. You can also find the complete checklist on their website.

General Characteristics of 2e Learners

- Appears smarter than grades or test scores suggest
- Has a sophisticated speaking vocabulary but poorer written expression
- Participates well in class discussions but does not follow through with implementation
- Has uneven academic skills, inconsistent grades, and test scores
- Does well when given sufficient time but performs poorly on timed tests and takes much longer to complete assignments and homework than other students
- Studies very hard before tests and earns good grades on tests but soon forgets most of the learned information. Needs to restudy it for later tests
- Has excellent problem-solving skills but suffers from low self-esteem
- Excels in one area or subject but may appear average in others
- Performs well with challenging work but struggles with easy material
- Is better with reading comprehension than with phonetic decoding of words
- Is better at math reasoning than computation
- Has wonderful ideas but has difficulty organizing tasks and activities
- Has facility with computers, but illegible or slow handwriting
- Has a great (sometimes bizarre) sense of humor and may use it to distract the class
- Thrives on complexity but has difficulty with rote memorization
- Understands concepts easily and gets frustrated with the performance requirements
- Fatigues easily due to the energy required to compensate

Chapter 1

Book Study & Reflection Questions

Based on the definition of twice-exceptionality, does this better help you understand your child? What attributes of 2e does your child have?

Consider the possibility that there is more you are not seeing. What else could be going on? How would you know?

Chapter 2
Some Familiar Names

Being a child who is twice-exceptional (2e) has many challenges. However, by focusing on the learner's strengths and using successful coping strategies, disabilities and challenges can be effectively managed. A 2e individual can certainly lead a successful life despite the issues they may struggle with.

What follows are a few examples of well-known people who have impacted many of our lives. The men and women we highlight in this chapter were successful individuals who were incredibly intelligent and talented but overcame significant obstacles.

Agatha Christie

Agatha Christie wrote 66 detective novels, 14 short story collections, the play *Mousetrap*, and six novels under the pseudonym Mary Westmacott. She was honored in the Guinness Book of World Records as the best-selling fiction writer of all time. But unknown to some, Agatha suffered from dysgraphia, a disorder that affects a person's ability to write and spell.

Agatha once said that writing and spelling were very difficult for her, and she was considered "slow" in school and by her family. However, she once stated in an interview that she found other ways to achieve her dream of becoming a writer. Her challenge with writing did not stop her from becoming a famous writer known worldwide.

Winston Churchill

Winston Churchill was the Prime Minister of Great Britain and the winner of the 1953 Nobel Prize in Literature. He served as the Prime Minister during World War II and from 1951 to 1955. He was best known for his wartime leadership and eloquent radio speeches, providing encouragement and inspiration to fight against the odds, no matter how bleak the future seemed.

Ironically, he suffered from a lisp, which was rumored to be more pronounced during stressful times. He compensated by doing speech exercises and slowing down while talking.

Walt Disney

Walt Disney was the creator of Disneyland, Walt Disney World, and many beloved films and animated characters, such as Mickey Mouse. He was an entrepreneur who became a great writer, animator, and film producer, among his many talents. He held the record for receiving the most Academy Awards and was presented with two Golden Globes and an Emmy. His fanciful creations are beloved by children around the world.

Walt had dyslexia, which can impact a person's reading, spelling, and writing abilities. As a child, he was considered "slow" and lost a newspaper job for what they called his "lack of creativity." Little did they know that this man would become one of the creators of the world's most loved fantasy places and characters.

Thomas Edison

Thomas Edison was an inventor and businessman developing a number of ideas and devices in electric power, mass communication, sound recordings, and film. He invented the concept of the phonograph and the early light bulb, which paved the way for the world of technology we know today. His use of the scientific method in his work and his collaboration with other researchers produced some remarkable inventions.

Edison suffered from hearing problems and was nearly deaf by age 12. His mother worked with him, teaching him the art of patience and perseverance. He remains one of our greatest and most prolific inventors.

Albert Einstein

Albert Einstein was a theoretical physicist. He developed the theory of relativity, creating his famous equation, "$E = mc^2$," and contributed to the theory of quantum mechanics. He received the 1921 Nobel Prize for Physics.

Albert is suspected of having some autistic traits, and many believe he may have also had ADHD due to his persistent struggles in school. He did not speak until he was three years old. However, his challenges did not prevent him from becoming one of the greatest physicists of all time.

Alexander Graham Bell

Alexander Graham Bell, who struggled with dyslexia, founded the Bell Telephone Company and invented the telephone. His grandfather and brother had done work in elocution and speech, and his mother and wife were deaf, resulting in Alexander's interest in working with hearing devices and acoustics.

He first experimented with a machine that could draw shapes based on sound waves. However, with his theory that metal reeds could be tuned to convert undulating currents into sound, he later expounded upon the telegraph and experimented with acoustic telegraphy. This ground-breaking experimentation resulted in the early telephone. Alexander was an excellent example of what someone can accomplish, despite their challenges.

Helen Keller

Helen Keller was a political activist and lecturer. She lost her sight and hearing as an infant. After meeting her teacher, Anne Sullivan, she learned language, reading, and writing through Braille and the Tadoma method, which involves touching someone's face to perceive their jaw movements.

She attended Radcliffe and Harvard and became the first deaf and blind person to earn a Bachelor of Arts Degree. She toured the world and advocated for persons with disabilities.

Howard Hughes

Howard Hughes was an investor, engineer, and pilot. As a pilot, he set several speed records in airplanes he had designed himself. In 1935, Howard set a speed record of over 352 miles per hour near California in a plane called the H-1 Racer. He would also contribute to the growth of transcontinental airlines and the use of modern jet planes.

Howard suffered from chronic pain caused by several plane crashes and demonstrated eccentric behavior believed to be Obsessive Compulsive Disorder (OCD). Despite these disabilities, he became highly influential and financially successful during most of his adult life.

Chapter 2

Did it surprise you that any of these people were on this list? Who stood out and why?

Can you think of any other well-known people who may likely be twice-exceptional? Who?

Why would it be important for our twice-exceptional children, or any child, to learn about some of these famous people?

Why is it necessary for teachers and parents to learn their stories?

Chapter 3
Where Are We?

Everywhere.

Twice-exceptional (2e) children are found in all schools and grade levels. 2e children become 2e adults, parents, uncles, aunts, and grandparents. There are three subgroups of 2e learners. Some have:

1. Gifts compensating for their disability(s)
2. A disability(s) overshadowing their gifts
3. Gifts and disability(s) masking each other

Within the educational setting, 2e learners are often identified as having gifted or special needs, with the latter being the more prevalent identification. Some children are identified in both areas and have all their needs met. Many are not identified in either area and use their own strategies to cope with school. Other 2e learners are puzzled about why and how they differ from peers, and they internalize the differences as character flaws.

Any child with a disability or challenge can be talented or gifted in another area. If you understand the gifted learner, you know they are not gifted in all domains and can still struggle in certain areas. The issue is that for students who have significant struggles and are gifted, where do they fit? How do parents and educators meet their needs? How might we meet all of their needs?

2e learners tend to be under-identified and require a unique level of servicing that the regular school system is often not equipped to identify and provide. This makes it even more difficult for these students. 2e learners can be found within every socio-economic, racial, and cultural background. When we consider that 2e learners can be found in every type of educational setting, how many 2e options are available in our schools? When looking at gifted programs and services, many schools have limited support for those learners, if any.

So, just how many children in our country are 2e? One 2006 study by the NEA estimated around 360-610,000 students might be 2e. Unfortunately, there is little overall data on what percentage of the gifted population is twice-exceptional. In fact, there are many issues in accurately determining the number of gifted students in the United States as, in the end, every state has its own definition of giftedness and how it is measured.

Based on quantitative data, we can only assume how many students formally fit into the 2e category. Linda Silverman, an eminent clinician of complex outliers, states that giftedness masks disabilities and disabilities depress intelligence test scores. The public school system currently has approximately 3.2 million gifted and talented students. Around 6 million students are also being served by the Individuals with Disabilities Act. With that in mind, it can be assumed that approximately 6% of this population is most likely gifted and talented based on the numbers.

There needs to be a more accurate way to identify 2e students, and then we can develop an appropriate program model to serve them.

Chapter 3

Book Study & Reflection Questions

Have you reached out to your child's school to learn what supports are available for areas of giftedness and areas of struggle?

Does your school have counselors and resources outside of class for students who need additional academic, social, and emotional support? Because schools are consistently struggling with a scarcity of resources, what can you do if they are lacking at your child's school? Brainstorm here.

Chapter 4
Problems We Face in a School Setting

The first problem these students face is having adults understand that they can be gifted or talented in one or more areas while simultaneously struggling in another area. **The second challenge is the ability of the school system to provide everyone with an education that meets their academic and emotional needs while assisting them in reaching their potential.**

Twice-exceptional means that a learner has both gifts and talents as well as a disability in one or more areas.

Let's begin with some disabilities these students may have. Some of the more common twice-exceptionalities are as follows:

- Learning Challenges

- Physical Challenges

- Sensory Challenges

- Autism Spectrum Disorder

- Emotional and Behavior Disorders

- AD/HD

- Dyslexia

According to the *Twice Exceptional Dilemma* from the National Education Association, twice-exceptional students often face the following challenges in the public school system:

1. Identified as gifted but not having an identified disability
   (gift compensates for disability)

2. Identified as having a disability but not an area of giftedness
   (disability overshadows gift)

3. Not identified as either, with one exceptionality masking the other
   (gift and disability mask each other)

The public school system is structured with three main ways to service children:

- The traditional route, which lends to the "average" student

- The special education route, which assists those students demonstrating a disability or challenge in their learning

- The gifted route, which serves students with an academic or other strength

The traditional assessments that are in place for these structures are not specifically equipped to discover a student with a dual, specialized diagnosis. In addition, educators and school administrators are often not given adequate training to identify or provide instruction to these students.

Families may also be unaware of their needs because they lack knowledge of the characteristics of a dual diagnosis and because of the ability of the gifted traits and disabilities to mask one another.

As a result, many twice-exceptional children are under-identified and are left to struggle on their own.

For instance, a student who has been identified as gifted but has an unidentified disability can struggle with the following issues:

- Self-esteem and motivational issues due to challenges in learning and misguided expectations by others

- Being labeled an underachiever based on lack of work or struggles with executive functioning*

- Lack of services or appropriate differentiation because of under-identified challenges

- Emotional and behavioral issues that surface because of the lack of support in the areas of need

*Higher level cognitive processes of planning, decision-making, problem-solving, action sequencing, task assignment and organization, effortful and persistent goal pursuit, inhibition of competing impulses, flexibility in goal selection, and goal-conflict resolution. - *American Psychological Association Dictionary*

Likewise, a student who has been identified with a disability but has not been identified as gifted has the following challenges:

- Boredom due to lack of challenge in areas of strength

- Test scores that do not adequately reflect strengths and giftedness

- Underserved talents and strengths due to a high level of remediation

- Low expectations of self, family, and educators

- Low self-esteem

- Learned helplessness

In some cases, students challenged in either of these scenarios may appear "typical" because they have learned to hide and accommodate their shortcomings.

In any case, 2e students need an appropriate education that assists them with their giftedness as well as disability or area of challenge.

Fortunately, this is becoming a more widely known area of need. More research is starting to focus on supporting students facing these challenges.

We are focusing on students who come into classrooms with challenges that coexist with their giftedness. We have an entire book with strategies on how to support gifted children. There is a summary of strategies on the following page.

Looking at these two areas of focus in one individual, we understand that these students genuinely need extra understanding and support.

Gifted & Trauma – 20 Things Adults Need to Know

From <u>Gifted Children & How Trauma Impacts Them</u> by Adam Laningham, Melissa Sadin, & Nathan Levy

1. Please Do Not Use The "G" Word With Me

2. Please Do Not Assume Labeling Me Will Help Me

3. Just Because I Have The Potential To Excel At Things Does Not Mean That I Will Want To

4. I Am Not A Tutor Or Teacher Assistant

5. Writing Is Sometimes Hard For Me

6. Sometimes I May Seem Lazy, But Other Times I Am Just Not Motivated

7. Just Because I Am Academically Above My Average Age Level Peers Does Not Mean I Am As Socially Mature As They Are

8. Just Because I Am Smart Does Not Mean I Am Organized

9. Sometimes I Just Know Things

10. I Still Need To Acquire Basic Knowledge

11. School Is Not Designed For Kids Like Me & Gifted Does Not Mean I Like Or Will Do Well In School

12. I Have My Passions That I Must Explore - I Do Not Know Why I Become Fixated On Certain Topics, Or Why My Interests Change

13. My Brain Is Motivated By Novelty

14. I Am The Most Engaged When I See The Big Picture

15. I Often Need True Differentiation

16. Please Do Not Stop Me From Questioning Things

17. I Need To Be Taught How To Think And Problem-Solve

18. Connections, Connections, Connections

19. Please Take A Breath, I Am Going To Be Just Fine

20. We Really Need The 50 / 50 Rule for Our Gifted Programs

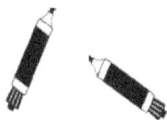

BRIGHT CHILD
— B O O K S —
www.BrightChildBooks.com

Find many more books or book a training on our website:

www.brightchildbooks.com

Chapter4

In what areas does your child excel?

Do they have many opportunities to participate in this area of strength regularly? List and reflect.

In what areas is your child struggling?

What have you found that seems to help in the challenge areas? How can these strategies be used to support in other areas?

Do you think his or her area of strength can be used to support in any areas of challenge? Brainstorm here.

Have you shared with the school any strategies that seem to help your child? If not, think about and reflect on a plan to share what you have learned.

Chapter 5
Complexities to Overcome When We Are in a Traditional School Setting

Understanding a child's needs can be quite frustrating when the child struggles at home and/or school. These children can seem very advanced one minute and then appear to struggle the next. Understanding this dichotomy and finding help and support is challenging when you have difficulty understanding or knowing the issue.

Parents face many complexities when it comes to raising twice-exceptional children. Over the years, we have noticed that the following are seen the most often:

Identification complexities - Identifying the actual needs of your child. The federal government does not mandate gifted programs; thus, they vary from state to state and even from school to school. Because special education is mandated by law, identifying 2e students as having special needs typically occurs much faster than recognizing their gifted potential. Areas of struggle requiring support may seem easier to identify than areas of strength by school personnel. Because of this, talents may be overlooked in the school setting because of the common use of a deficiency-based model.

Curriculum complexities - Because the content of gifted programs is determined by the state, the district, or in some cases, even the individual school, not all programs are as rigorous as they could be. Not all teachers are trained to facilitate learning for gifted students. In many cases, they are not equipped to handle the unique needs of 2e students in the classroom. **It is vital for parents to understand how best to advocate for their children. Always lead with their strengths!** Although supporting a 2e child's challenges is very important, the primary focus for any 2e child's education should not begin in an area of challenge but in an area of strength.

Social and emotional complexities - Twice-exceptional children can be sensitive learners with complex needs. They can become easily frustrated, have their self-esteem plummet, or become isolated because of misunderstandings. We must facilitate twice-exceptional children to become self-aware and eventually advocate for their own needs.

Teachers also have to be trained to meet the needs of these complex learners. This is nothing new; however, the social climate seems to be making things more difficult for our classroom educators.

Because schools are under more pressure, scrutiny, and stress, identifying and serving twice-exceptional students is becoming more challenging. Since the pandemic of 2020, we have seen many experienced educators leave the system. With them goes a wealth of knowledge and expertise that is difficult to replace.

Currently, many schools are seeing significant teacher turnover and vacancies. When younger, less-experienced teachers are hired, school administrators must spend more time training them on the basics of conventional teaching. This leaves precious little time for the specialized training that is needed to teach our children with more complex learning needs.

Unfortunately, with limited resources and expertise, the odds of your child being in a classroom with a teacher who has been trained in gifted strategies and scaffolding student needs is relatively low. It has never been more critical for parents of our twice-exceptional learners to be involved with their child's education. Emphasis should be placed on developing a relationship with your child's teacher to support your child. You may even have to learn together. That is fine if you are both open and willing to place your child's unique needs first.

Teaching is still considered a noble profession, and exceptional people still become teachers. Your teacher may not yet have the specific tools ready to help your child, but working together is the key to supporting your child's education.

Chapter 5

Book Study & Reflection Questions

What are some of the struggles you are facing now regarding your child's educational environment?

What steps have you taken to address them?

Take a moment to consider possible solutions to other challenges you and your child are facing.

Chapter 6
Successful Strategies for Our Parents

Having a child who falls under the twice-exceptional umbrella can be wonderful, as well as confusing and frustrating. It is important that you educate yourself on twice-exceptional characteristics and understand how they apply to your unique child. Take time to really get to know your child. **You are your child's best advocate**. Be open to how they see and perceive things, and remember that all children need to be challenged and supported in a way that is best for them. Confronting challenges with adequate support is a good thing.

Parents should research and experiment to find successful strategies and programs that work well with these types of learners and then observe how their child reacts and excels, or struggles, with these elements. Keep anecdotal records and examples of your child's experiences to show to school staff or counselors to discuss programs or point out things that are working well. Be willing to ask for extensions or modifications to assignments when needed. Most teachers are happy to help support your child.

We cannot emphasize enough that **you always want to try to work in partnership with your child's school.** Working in collaboration with teachers is an ideal way to see the whole picture of your child's learning. You can share challenges and accomplishments during homelife, and teachers can share what they see during the school day. Children often behave differently in various environments. They can also view situations differently. Working with the other adults who spend time with your child can help you understand your child much better.

Remember that as your child progresses through school, some teachers will have different teaching styles, expectations, and ways of running their classrooms. We have all had teachers we loved and those we did not. That is okay. This is part of the learning experience that prepares children for adulthood. As long as the school and teacher are willing to work with you to help your child, working with them is usually the best option when things get tough.

You always want your child to see that you are working with the teacher, and you both want what is best for them. Even if you disagree with the teacher, you do not want your child to see it. A split, or even a perceived split, between you and the teacher, can cause more problems. We have seen many children over the years use these divisions to avoid doing work or to act out negatively. (More on this is discussed in the following chapter.)

Understand your rights and responsibilities as a parent, and know what plans and programs for gifted students and students with disabilities are available. Twice-exceptional students may need both programs to expand on their strengths and to cope with their challenges. Do not let their disabilities overshadow their gifted areas. Children must be encouraged to spend time working in their areas of interest. When they do not have these opportunities, depression, anxiety, and other mental health challenges can emerge. The same can happen if their disabilities are overlooked. Burnout may be around the corner when students are repeatedly asked to do difficult things without needed supports.

Network with agencies and other families. Join the school's parent groups and check out your local gifted organizations. There are a number of gifted and twice-exceptional parent discussion forums online where you can learn from others who have similar lived experiences with their children. Just keep an open mind and do not get drawn into negativity.

Become familiar with the teachers and specialists at school and other advocates in your school's district. Other outside groups, such as non-profits and federal programs, can also help. The SENG (Supporting the Emotional Needs of the Gifted)

Model Parent Groups are a wonderful place to meet parents with shared experiences. It can be a valuable resource if you can join a local group in person or find one online.

Lastly, **take time for yourself.** It is not a selfish thing to do. Being an advocate can be challenging and exhausting. You need time to recharge and recoup. If you are stressed out, you will not be as effective in your advocacy role for your child. Remember, your child is always watching you and learning from your actions and how you respond to difficult things.

Parent Checklist for 2e Support

1. Be open about your child's unique needs

2. Have your child assessed and learn their strengths and areas where support is needed

3. When it comes to supporting your child, lead with their strengths (NEST)

4. Evaluate the programs at your child's school

5. Work as a team with the school, but do not be afraid to advocate for your child

6. Help your child to sharpen social skills and find appropriate extracurricular activities

7. Allow them to struggle productively and encourage them in their endeavors

8. Talk to other parents and educate yourself

9. Take time for yourself

Twice-Exceptional Children - From Struggling to Thriving

Chapter 6

What steps have you already taken from our checklist? Highlight them on the checklist. What are your next steps in supporting your child?

What is the next step for you to take? How are you going to take this step?

Choose one of the **bolded** phrases from this chapter and reflect on its significance.

Chapter 7
What Can a Parent Do if the School is Not Supportive of Their Child's Needs?

Please remember that teachers will have different teaching styles, expectations, and ways of running their classrooms as your child moves through school. Again, we have all worked with special teachers we still remember and others we quickly forgot. As long as the school and teacher are willing to work with you to help your child, collaboration is usually the best option when issues arise.

Additionally, you always want your child to see that you are working with the teacher and that you both want what is best for them. You do not want your child to see a rift between you and the teacher, leaving them to wonder who has their best interests in mind. This can lead to some children using the divisions to act out, avoid work, or seek attention from it. **Even if you are frustrated, always show your child that the**

adults in their life are working as a team to support them.

If there comes a point when you have been working with the teacher, and your child is still not having success, it is best to work with the counselors, support staff, and administration to see what can be done. A school thinking of a student's best needs will work with you to help find solutions.

Many laws are available to support parents with students with learning disabilities. The Individuals with Disabilities Education Act (IDEA) is a law that makes available a free and appropriate public education to eligible children with disabilities throughout the nation and ensures special education and related services to those children. An individualized education program or IEP is a written statement for each child with a disability that is developed, reviewed, and revised in a meeting in accordance with various statutes and must include a list of support areas and goals.

If your child has an IEP, work with your child's IEP team if they are not receiving the services they need, or you are not seeing progress. If you feel your child may need an IEP, you should contact the local public school to begin the process. You will also have to do some research on your own, as this can be a lengthy process, and you may choose to use psychological assessment services outside of the school.

Alternatively, students with health concerns or disabilities may receive a 504 support plan through their public school. Looking into how these legal supports can help you is a good idea if you have been working with the teachers and school and things are not improving.

As for giftedness, those laws vary from state to state. Many 2e children are found because of their areas of weakness, but their giftedness may go unfound and unserved. If your child is in this situation, prompt the school team to ensure their strengths are supported as well. You may need to ask your child's IEP team to include your child's strengths in the IEP or even the 504 plan.

If your school will not work with you or you have realized the school is not a good long-term fit, do your homework and look at your options. Most states permit some form of school choice to allow parents to select enrollment in other district schools. Many states have charter school options, and private schools may be a consideration for those who can afford them.

Additionally, online schooling or homeschooling with online support is growing in popularity. There are many online parent groups to support you and your child in this situation. Please remember that you will lose in-person opportunities for school support and socialization for your child. Therefore, think this through carefully if this is an option you are considering.*

We explain how to use the simple yet effective T-Chart for decision-making in Chapter 8. You may want to skip ahead, look, and see if this tool would be helpful as you make your decision. We have left space on page 88.

Unfortunately, not all schools know how to, nor want to, engage in helping this unique population. For many educators, this is simply a new concept for them. It is a bit of a paradox when a child who is so advanced in one area struggles profoundly in another.

These children's needs may simply go unnoticed by some educators, especially if they are new to the profession. Giftedness, in particular, often receives little attention in general college teacher preparation courses, and it may go unmentioned in special education courses. When teachers have not received specialized training in gifted strategies, they will unlikely understand how to provide an appropriate education to twice-exceptional students.

Despite these things, we always recommend working with your child's teacher first. If your child is struggling, the teacher will most impact their progress. Even if you do not see eye to eye, it is always best to share your concerns, allow them time to work with your child, and then check back for a progress update. It is reasonable to request weekly or bi-weekly updates on your child and to share any new progress you see at home.

Chapter 7

Book Study & Reflection Questions

What have you done to build a good working relationship with your child's teacher and school this year?

When a concern arises in the future, what is your plan to address it?

There is no perfect school. However, if your child continues to struggle after you have worked with the teachers and school staff, you may want to check out other school options that may serve as a better educational fit. – You may not be ready to move your child now, but it is good to know what is out there if you see a pattern of struggle from your child.

If you are considering another schooling option for your child, you can start the thinking process here.

1. Where is your child now?

_____

Positives/Benefits	Negatives (or Possible drawback

2.   Another possible educational setting:

_____

Positives/Benefits	Negatives (or Possible drawbacks)

3.   Another possible educational setting:

_____

Positives/Benefits	Negatives (or Possible drawbacks)

Chapter 8

Empowering Parents to Make Home Education Decisions

Parents choose home education, aka homeschooling, for various reasons. Home education can bring great freedom in subject choices, content depth, delivery, teacher-facilitator, length of learning periods, mode of learning, and scheduling of learning periods. On the other hand, with the rapid ever-expanding options available, it can be overwhelming for parents to be the principal, administrator, and teacher of their child's home education.

Home education can take different forms for individual families. The following are the major categories:

- Traditional (Traditional Schooling Methods)
- Eclectic (Child-Centered)
- Unschooling (Child-Driven)
- Worldschooling (Experiential-Learning through Interaction with our World)

Cinder's Tale: Reluctant Home Education to Radical Acceleration
(A parent's experience in a fairytale format)

Once upon a time, a bright child named Cinder knew she was different from most of her schoolmates. Because she was academically high performing and often sat quietly reading at her desk, no one thought anything was amiss. Cinder wondered what the purpose of school was and why she had to wait to explore topics of interest to her.

Powerful people told her that she had to be a good girl and wait until high school to explore topics she was interested in - what was the rush to examine issues meant for much older learners? They believed she was far too young to understand such things. Her only option was to read at school after finishing her work. Although she loved reading, she soon exhausted the reading materials deemed suitable by the powerful people. What was she to do?

Cinder and her parents reluctantly embarked on one year of home education. This choice was made out of despair because Cinder's essence, spark, curiosity, and soul were dying day by day. Home education was the fairy godmother for Cinder and her parents. Cinder was finally able to explore and engage in exciting classes. She experimented with different class formats - from virtual, discussion-based, small-group, year-long classes to short and intense community college courses.

Cinder's family saw her transform from a painfully shy girl who retreated into her own world into one who expressed her thoughts and feelings about her education. Through the freedom to experiment with learning, Cinder discovered that her preferred educational environment included small, in-person classes taught in a college format of few and intense classes in logic, math, statistics, art, economics, and problem-solving.

Eventually, she chose to radically accelerate, skipping high school altogether. Because of her increased confidence, she was able to independently live in a college dorm far, far away from her family at 14 years old. She finally found her Goldilocks Zone, a place that matched course pacing and exploration better, stretching herself with greater choices and depth in learning.

Operating in her Goldilocks Zone within a safe environment allowed Cinder to spread her wings to grow academically, psychologically, and emotionally into a whole person with greater resilience and well-being. Her relationship with her family grew closer despite being physically farther apart.

What is going through your mind as you read this true story? Finding your child's Goldilocks Zone can be transformational. Remember that it is a zone (range), not a fixed spot or state. The Goldilocks Zone changes dynamically over time, reacting to your child's experience to internal (e.g., biology, neurology, psychology) and external (e.g., environmental, cultural, relational) interactions.

Thinking Routines

The following are some thinking routines to guide you through various considerations to help you make intentional home education choices that support and nurture your child's curiosity, interests, and strengths. At the same time, challenges that might get in the way must always be considered.

Using a **holistic lens** includes thinking about your child as a whole person **and** your family values and goals as you consider the following:

1. **Subject choices:**
   Are there non-negotiables? Make sure subject selections always include subjects of interest and strength. How do challenges impact subject choices? Does your child learn thematically based on interest?

2. Content depth:

Is it at the right level? Are there any factors you need to consider that may impact the depth of curricula?

3. Mode of learning and delivery method:

Does your child prefer online learning for specific subjects and content? Other learning options include was such as experiential, hands-on, virtual, conversational, one-on-one, small group, and observational learning and delivery.

4. Teacher-facilitator:

Who will be teaching various subjects or content? What role does the teacher play? Are some subjects better learned through a facilitation role versus direct instruction? Is your child sensitive to learner-educator relationships?

5. Length of learning periods:

What length of learning period makes sense for your child? Perhaps different subjects require different amounts of time for study.

6. Scheduling of learning periods:

Which part of the day should you schedule various learning periods?

Be flexible, experiment, and be ready to change as your child grows and develops. Involve your child in providing feedback and use it to continuously refine the learning plan.

T-Charts - Free, Flexible, and Visual
The following section includes one of our favorite practical low-tech, no-cost, highly flexible visual mapping strategies - T-charts.

T-charts help guide you and your child's thinking around routines, preferences, environments, and curriculum.

Why we love T-charts:

- It helps to foster a psychologically and emotionally neutral space when we discuss sensitive and complex topics such as strengths and challenges, likes and dislikes. When you and your child are having discussions focused on items in the T-chart, there is a shared connection and sense that all parties are equally involved; all parties are important stakeholders and are valued for their perspectives.

- It helps to track changes over time visually. You can share T-charts with other stakeholders involved in supporting your child's success.

- A chart is a concrete way to help foster flexible problem-solving, communication, and reframing from a deficit-focused to a strength-nurturing perspective, as illustrated by the example below.

Taking Stock - Practical Strategies You Can Use Now

T-Chart
Many uses – Examples:
1. Used to know your child better
2. Advocating appropriate learning environments in school
3. Self-efficacy entry point

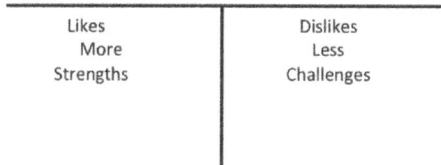

Likes More Strengths	Dislikes Less Challenges

An example: More and Less

Make a list with your child under each section using "more" and "less."

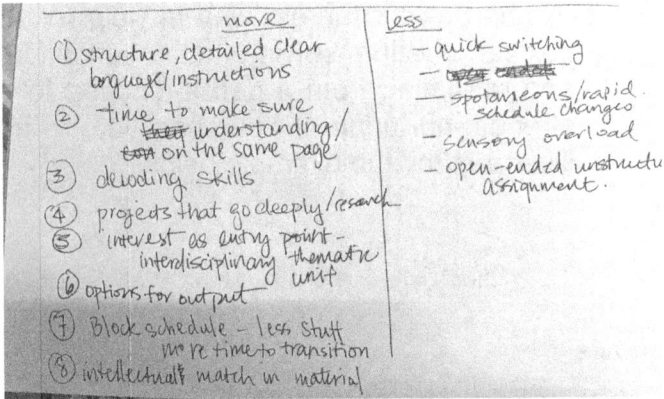

more	less
① structure, detailed clear language/instructions	– quick switching
② time to make sure ~~that~~ understanding / ~~that~~ on the same page	– ~~rigid~~ ~~endles~~
	– spontaneous/rapid schedule changes
③ decoding skills	– sensory overload
④ projects that go deeply / research	– open-ended unstructu assignment.
⑤ interest as entry point – interdisciplinary thematic unit	
⑥ options for output	
⑦ Block schedule – less stuff more time to transition	
⑧ intellectual match in material	

After you are done, look at your list; consider moving items between the "more" and "less" sections in your T-chart to maximize strengths and minimize, scaffold, or bypass challenges.

Other ways to use T-charts:

1. They may be used as entry points to gauge any discrepancy between your and your child's perceptions of their strengths and challenges.

2. You and your child could both complete a T-chart together to share each other's strengths and challenges, showing your 2e

child that everyone has areas of strengths and challenges.

3. Keep a series of T-charts over time to help document changes. Are you moving towards utilizing more strengths, enjoying success, and creating greater awareness and understanding for yourself and your child?

Chapter 8

Book Study & Reflection Questions

Use the T-chart to weigh the benefits and challenges of homeschooling your child.

Positives/Benefits	Negatives (or Possible drawbacks)

What can you do to address some of the foreseen challenges?

What resources have you found to support you in your homeschooling endeavors?

How will you support your child's social and emotional needs if you decide to homeschool? (You can refer to Chapters 9 & 10 for more information on their importance.)

Chapter 9
How Extracurricular Activities Can Help Us

All over and as much as can be provided.

Extracurricular activities can provide transitional recreation services that help build independence in classroom settings, including those that support leisure and social skills. Benefits may be gained from after-school programs, summer camps, community programs, etc. It is helpful for twice-exceptional students to find success in multiple areas. Activities outside of the classroom are vital for real-world learning and build self-confidence as well as socialization skills.

Some extracurricular programs may address a student's academic, communication, vocational, or social goals and can be included in an educational plan.

Art and Music

Art and music can provide therapeutic outlets for communicating thoughts and feelings. Creativity can be expressed in many different forms by all types of students. Allowing a student to demonstrate knowledge of a subject creatively empowers them and will enable educators to understand what the person truly knows.

Music has been known to increase executive functioning by providing training through rhythm and performance. Through regular practice of an instrument or voice, a healthy routine may be established. Many 2e students can express themselves creatively through different forms of music.

Performing Arts

Acting and drama have many academic, social, and collaborative benefits for 2e students. Critical analysis of a production and script can provide a deeper understanding of the author's characters, message, and purpose. Multiple script readings can help build fluency, accuracy, vocabulary development, and intonation. Acting can provide an opportunity for students to express themselves artistically and can help build confidence and tenacity. Collaborating with other children through teamwork in the performing arts often helps improve communication and interpersonal relationships.

Improvisation is also an excellent activity for students to try as long as the teacher is sensitive to shy participants. True improv is a collaborative effort where all participants can have fun and appreciate each other's creativity.

Sports/Athletics

Engagement in sports can lead to a better self-image and an improved understanding of collaboration and teamwork. Sports can assist students in learning new skills, including visual-spatial and even mathematical, while they enjoy the benefits of exercise and relaxation. Participating in sports can aid in social-emotional development as well. Competitive sports can foster a growth mindset by allowing students to learn through mistakes. Team sports are also valuable in adding teamwork skills and relationship building.

Finding enriching extracurricular activities for your child is important. Let children explore and find activities that interest them. It may take some time. Different activities can be explored until you find the right one or two that genuinely engage your child. A music tutor, a local book club, Boy or Girl Scouts, and many other things can provide a positive outlet.

Chapter 9

Book Study & Reflection Questions

What activities outside of school does your child enjoy?

What activities can your child participate in that allows them to shine?

What activities can your child do that might connect to other areas of struggle?

Are there activities your whole family can participate in together where you can model growth and resiliency?

Chapter 10
The Importance of Mindfulness, Social, & Emotional Supports

Twice-exceptional children can have social and emotional issues that interfere with their ability to make friends and sustain social relationships. These issues can prevent them from providing themselves with self-care and to manage themselves successfully in stressful situations.

In addition to this, 2e students may have emotional issues tied to their academic and social challenges, such as feelings of failure, depression, anger, isolation, self-harm, and, in extreme cases, suicide. Students need tools in order to overcome these issues. Opportunities to develop a healthy self-awareness, identify their own vulnerabilities, and interact with other students who share in their struggles are often helpful.

This can be done through:

1. Journaling and Creating Positive Rituals

Start a morning or evening routine by participating in relaxation exercises, goal setting, or inspirational activities, along with identifying one's current state of mind and needs. This could be done by writing questions or affirmations about oneself in a journal. Looking back on some of the entries and celebrating current accomplishments from past ideas can increase positivity.

2. Maintain Emotional Well-Being

Provide oneself with opportunities for meditation, or mind-clearing, as this can be an emotionally cleansing experience. Watching the sunset, participating in breathing exercises, sitting outside, coloring, or listening to the wind are all great activities for this. Surrounding oneself with supportive, positive people is also vital to maintaining mental stability, as is minimizing interactions with critical or negative peers.

3. Self-Check In

During the day, provide oneself with a check-in and assess current feelings.

Ask these questions:

- What are you thinking?

- Are you having physical reactions to stress or thoughts?

- What could you do to minimize any negative feelings or thoughts?

All of these can be done at home or in the classroom. Just taking a "Mindful Moment" when students come in from lunch or PE can profoundly change the energy in the classroom. Students do not have to meditate; simply taking one or two full minutes to close their eyes and clear their minds is a great mental break. You can even use a chime, a singing bowl, or a peaceful melody to start the moment.

Another tool is to use seating and tactile objects to support fidgeting and help with focus. These can be stress balls, glitter sticks, or other tactile sensory toys (easily found online) to help with fidgeting. Purchasing or making wiggle seats, allowing students to sit on yoga balls, and using standing desks (or something as simple as two cut tennis balls to place on chair feet, allowing a quiet way to wiggle) can help students focus. Large rubber bands can even be placed on chair legs to allow feet and legs to bounce quietly.

Using accommodations shows you are open to ensuring they are comfortable and ready to learn.

Many of these tools will help children focus. If you are worried about them becoming toys, you can have that conversation and say they will lose the privilege of using them for a while if they become a distraction. Once the novelty wears off, the initial issues will fade.

Please Don't Forget That…
You are important too!

Being a caretaker for the people you love is challenging and stressful. Your mental state and stability are just as important as your child's well-being. Stress and fatigue significantly impact your emotional and physical health, and you must treat yourself with kindness and self-respect. Here are a few ideas for you to achieve your own inner peace and balance:

1. Practice deep breathing and meditation

2. Take a warm shower or use a warm compress on the forehead

3. Listen to music or walk in nature

4. Read a book or watch a movie

5. Get a massage

6. Spend time with people you love

7. Take a break from news and technology

Chapter 10

Book Study & Reflection Questions

What "tools" can you provide your child at home to help them focus?

Ask your child what helps them focus. Jot their answers down here, then share some of the tools we discussed. Are they interested in trying any of them? Pinpoint one or two that may be of interest. Perhaps trying them at home first would be a good idea.

Chapter 11

What If I Need Someone Else to Talk To? How to Choose the Right Therapist for Your Child

We know some may hesitate to seek professional help, and others do not know what is available, where to start, or who to trust. We hope this section provides you with some answers. Our friend Jamie Dana, owner of Elevate Counseling in Phoenix, Arizona, provided this information.

The Right Counselor Can Foster Resilience and Growth

As many as one in six children have a diagnosable Mental Health Disorder (JAMA Pediatrics). Finding the right counselor to guide these children through the growing pains of childhood and adolescence can dramatically improve their chances of success in life. It is often comforting for parents deciding whether to invest time and money into a counselor to be reminded that mental illness is not a "choice" or a "moral failing." In fact, mental illnesses such as Anxiety, Mood Disorders, and ADHD occur at similar rates worldwide, in every culture, and among all socio-economic groups.

Therapy is about EMPOWERMENT, not INADEQUACY

If you are concerned that your child is experiencing a mental health problem, substance abuse, or a social struggle that is too big for them to handle on their own, the best time to address your concern is *now*.

The analogy of a young tree jettisoning to the side and then being corrected skywards again by a sturdy stake may be an appropriate comparison with counseling. Research shows that early intervention, with effective therapy, not only increases children's recovery rates but also builds resiliency and provides them with the skillsets needed to handle future stressors.

Choosing A Therapist

Finding a therapist may not be as easy as finding a good dentist or tutor. Because of the confidential nature of therapeutic relationships, many people are hesitant to share their positive (or negative) experiences in therapy openly. Luckily, there are many other ways for a savvy parent to begin the search for a counselor.

A good place to start is through trusted friends, a doctor, or the gifted specialist at your child's school. Typically, professionals who work with children in healthcare and education keep referral lists of specialists in the mental health arena. Another useful resource is PsychologyToday.com, where you can search by city, insurance company coverage, and specialty. If you are comfortable, crowdsourcing on social media by asking for therapy recommendations or searching previous posts (especially in a parenting group) can also prove effective.

Of course, many parents are limited to what their insurance covers. Unfortunately, in our experience, we have found that lists of approved counselors provided by insurance companies are not always updated. Sorting through these lists and contacting the providers for coverage and availability options may take considerable time. It is common for therapists to be booked one to four weeks out. Avoid allowing the vetting process to discourage you from finding a suitable counselor who fits your needs.

Once you have received several possible recommendations, reviewing the therapist's websites and bios is helpful. Many therapists will have additional information such as their background, education, specialties, accepted insurance, and session rates.

Experience Matters

Choose a counselor with experience and expertise in the areas that your child is struggling. For instance, if your child exhibits intense ruminations or repetitive behaviors, a mental health expert who works with kids and specializes in Obsessive-Compulsive Disorders would be helpful. Or if your teen is overly anxious, perfectionistic, and hard on themselves, meeting with an expert in high-functioning anxiety is important. If you have a child struggling with impulse control, organizing/planning, and social inhibition, finding an ADHD specialist will likely prove beneficial. Although there will be some crossover, each specialist will have additional training and tools in their proverbial toolboxes specifically designed to help your child handle their struggles.

Second, ensure that the specialist *also* has a good understanding of the unique needs of the gifted individual or a willingness to learn about giftedness. An effective therapist will be interested and open to learning more about the unique needs impacting the treatment of 2e kids, such as asynchronous development* and emotional intensities.

> *"Gifted children often have substantial variations in abilities within themselves and develop unevenly across various skill areas… because it is prominent in so many gifted children, some professionals believe asynchronous development, rather than potential or ability, is the defining characteristic of giftedness" (Webb, 2007). The original definition of asynchronous development was developed by The Columbus Group in 1991:*

> *Giftedness is asynchronous development in which advanced cognitive abilities and heightened intensity combine to create inner experiences and awareness that are qualitatively different from the norm. This asynchrony increases with higher intellectual capacity. The uniqueness of the gifted renders them particularly vulnerable and requires modifications in parenting, teaching, and counseling in order for them to develop optimally.*

Involve Your Child In The Process

After you have researched and vetted a couple of referrals for counselors, show the options to your child, and let them decide who would be a good fit for them. This gives your child a semblance of control. You are essentially saying, "You need to talk to someone, but I will let you decide who." It also bodes better for treatment outcomes. When a child or adult is open and engaged in treatment, they will be more invested and benefit more from the experience.

One note: your child may need to meet with a few therapists before you find the winning combination. Hold on to the list of additional options just in case the relationship doesn't click or falls flat. Sometimes this happens. (Do not worry; we, as therapists, understand and want the best for your family)! One of the most critical factors in recovery rates is feeling a strong connection to your counselor or therapist.

Support Your Child
By Building Your Reserves

If your child is struggling with maintaining emotional balance, there is a good chance that you are too. Unfortunately, these kinds of tensions can feed off of each other. You may be unintentionally making things worse. Consider getting support to improve your communication skills, develop strategies for de-escalation, cope with teen angst and rebellion, or better connect with your family. You will likely find that changing your behavior and attitude will also impact the rest of the family.

Life will throw many challenges at our kids, some requiring outside support. Therapy can help empower our children to develop the tools to build resilience, utilize coping strategies, and shift their mindset to lean into opportunities for growth.

The contribution of this chapter is provided by
Jamie Dana of Elevate Counseling
admin@elevatecounselingaz.com
https://elevatecounselingaz.com

Chapter 11

Book Study & Reflection Questions

Reflect on what you have read. Do you think your child needs outside help? How would you know?

If so, do you know where to turn? Some state gifted groups, national gifted organizations (such as SENG & NAGC), or state departments of education often have lists of mental health professionals.

Chapter 12
Above All Else: Don't Forget That I Am Gifted First!

As previously noted, if a 2e child is identified for support, it is most likely for help in their area(s) of challenge. Most school systems focus resources on identifying and supporting struggling students. A 2e student's high abilities can be overlooked with this deficit-based focus.

In many schools, support for an area of challenge is the only specific support students are provided. How will children excel if their area of strength is not nurtured?

A note from Adam – My first year of teaching was as a reading intervention teacher. Since I was new, I did what I was told and ran the program as it had always been done. The program was to support middle school students who were reading below grade level.

I had, and continue to have, concerns over how these programs are structured. The problem is that my intervention was during the student's elective class period. This meant that, instead of attending an elective of their choice, students would come to my classroom for extra reading support.

Just imagine if you were a child in this position. You are struggling in a particular area, and to "help you," we take you out of the class you enjoy. During this time, you do more work in the subject where you struggle the most. This seems like more of a punishment than a benefit to the child. What does this do to a child's motivation in school, especially for a child with a significant learning disability, as a 2e student might have?

Twice-exceptional children are gifted too. They have at least one area or talent in which they excel and one or more areas of disability. Both areas must be addressed to help these children succeed. Remember, 2e children are green, a distinct combination of yellow (strengths) and blue (disabilities).

In an ideal school district, the gifted and special education leaders work closely to support these students. In fact, in some districts, a child's giftedness comes first. What does this mean? It means a student is placed into gifted services and programming according to their needs. Special education then provides support within the gifted program structure. What does this look like?

There are many examples, and every school is different. One example may be quantitatively gifted children who excel in math but struggle with reading. These students can "walk up" to the next grade level for math for part of the school day, but for reading, the special education teacher can support their English Language Arts period in the classroom. These children can excel in math, the area of strength, and get the reading support they need. Students can feel fulfilled and successful in their domains of strength.

Where to Start?

If identifying all gifted students is not occurring at your school, you should start asking questions. Often parents need to bring awareness of 2e populations to their schools.

What can you do as a parent?

- Join local (district, school, state) gifted and 2e associations. What if there are no school gifted-related associations? Seek like-minded parents and form a group at your child's school.

- Through volunteering, you will get to know your teachers, administrators, and coordinators. Build your team of supporters and cheerleaders for your child.

- Attend board or trustee meetings to become informed and bring up your concerns. If your concerns represent a group, mobilize those parents to attend.

- Become familiar with your district's gifted and special education policy.

- Become familiar with your state's gifted and special education mandates.

Chapter 12

Book Study & Reflection Questions

Is your child's giftedness or area of strength being addressed? If not, how can you work with the school to ensure it happens?

If your child's areas of strength or giftedness cannot be addressed at school, what outside activities can they participate in to enjoy those experiences?

References, Articles, & Resources

Books –

Gifted Children & How Trauma Impacts Them: 20 Things Gifted Children Wish Their Teachers and Parents Understood
Adam C. Laningham, Dr. Melissa Sadin, & Nathan Levy, 2019

C for Curiosity
Lin Lim, Ph.D., 2022

Teachers' Guide to Trauma: 20 Things Kids with Trauma Wish Their Teachers Knew
Dr. Melissa Sadin & Nathan Levy, 2019

A Parent's Guide to Gifted Children
James T. Webb, Janet L. Gore, Edward R. Amend, & Arlene R. DeVries, 2007

Teacher's Guide to Resiliency Through The Arts
Cally Flox, Melisa Sadin, & Nathan Levy, 2019

Differentiation for Gifted Learners: Going Beyond the Basics

Diane Heacox & Richard M. Cash, 2020

The Power of Self-Advocacy for Gifted Learners: Teaching the Four Essential Steps to Success

Deb Douglas, 2017

What to do When Your Kid is Smarter Than You

Linda Levitt, 2007

Multiple Intelligences in the Elementary Classroom: A Teachers Toolkit

Susan Baum, Julie Viens, & Barbara Slatin, 2005

Understanding Twice-exceptional Learners: Connecting Research to Practice

Matthew Fugate, Wendy Behrens, & Cecelia Boswell, 2020

Twice Exceptional: Supporting and Educating Bright and Creative Students with Learning Difficulties
Scott Barry Kaufman (Ed.), 2018

Ungifted: Intelligence Redefined
Scott Barry Kaufman, 2015

The Explosive Child
Dr. Ross Greene, 2014

To Be Gifted and Learning Disabled: Strength-Based Strategies for Helping Twice-Exceptional Students With LD, ADHD, ASD, and More
Susan M. Baum, Robin Schader, & Steven Owen, 2017

Web Resources & Articles –

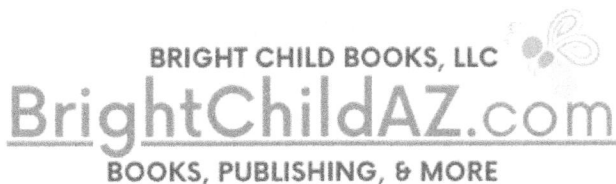

BRIGHT CHILD BOOKS, LLC

BrightChildAZ.com

BOOKS, PUBLISHING, & MORE

Check out the official website for this book and our series. We will be continually adding updated information, resources, presentations, etc.

https://brightchildbooks.com/collections/gifte d-struggling_twice-exceptional

ZENLIVING.COM
Lifespan Health

www.zenliving.com

SENG - Supporting Emotional Needs of the Gifted
www.sengifted.org

Bridges Graduate School of Cognitive Diversity in Education - Certificate, Master's and Doctoral Program **https://graduateschool.bridges.edu/**

www.2enews.com and Variations 2e magazine are focused on providing the latest news, research, and perspectives on how best to support the needs of this population of learners. Bridges 2e Center: Strength-based assessment to supplement IEP or 504 plan. Free resources, including monthly crucial conversations around 2e topics. **https://2ecenter.org/**

Ten tips for Teaching Twice-Exceptional Students ASCD **http://www.ascd.org/publications/newsletters/education_update/nov13/vol55/num11/Ten_Tips_for_Teaching_the_Twice-Exceptional_Student.aspx**

Strategies for Supporting Students who are Twice-Exceptional. The Journal of Special Education. **https://files.eric.ed.gov/fulltext/EJ1185416.pdf**

2eminds. Quick and Easy Mindfulness Practices
https://www.2eminds.com/mindfulness-parenting-twice-exceptional-2e-children/

gifted
development center
embracing giftedness

www.gifteddevelopment.org

The Columbus Organization
www.columbusorg.com

National Association for Gifted Children-
www.nagc.org

Your state Gifted Association

We also want to thank Jamie Dana again for her insight and contribution to Chapter 11.

Elevate Counseling
admin@elevatecounselingaz.com
https://elevatecounselingaz.com

About the Authors

Adam Chase Laningham, M.Ed
Consultant, Author, and
Founder of Bright Child AZ &
The Gifted Collective

Adam Laningham, author of Gifted Children & How Trauma Impacts Them and Thinkology 2.0, has over 20 years of experience in the field of education. Adam was recognized as the Arizona Gifted Teacher of the Year. He has taught at several schools in multiple grade levels, created and facilitated numerous gifted programs, and served as a district gifted services manager coordinating programs for over 6000 gifted students.

Adam has served on the Board of Directors for the Arizona Association for Gifted & Talented, is currently the President-Elect of SENG (Supporting the Emotional Needs of the Gifted), is a founding member of Callisto (supporting gifted foster youth), and an advisor for CogAT Riverside Insights. As founder and owner of Bright Child AZ, Adam is an international speaker, consultant, and gifted advocate.

www.brightchildaz.com

adam@brightchildbooks.com

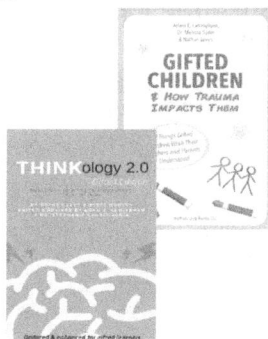

BRIGHT CHILD BOOKS, LLC
BrightChildAZ.com
BOOKS, PUBLISHING, & MORE

About the Authors

Lin Lim, Ph.D.
Dean of Graduate Students &
Translational Human
Development Scientist

Lin Lim is the Dean of Students and Communications at Bridges Graduate School of Cognitive Diversity in Education (BGS). She holds a doctorate in psychology from Boston University, an Academic Graduate Certificate in Mind, Brain, and Education (Johns Hopkins University), and an Academic Graduate Certificate in 2e Education (BGS).

Her current interests include interdisciplinary embodied complex dynamic systems thinking and practical applications around positive parenting, education, school-workplace transitions, and human development. She founded **Quark Collaboration Institute**, a non-profit focusing on human dignity and well-being across the lifespan. She serves on the boards of several gifted-related non-profits - Supporting the Emotional Needs of the Gifted (**SENG**), National Association for Gifted Children Parent Editorial Content and Advisory Board, Gifted Homeschoolers Forum (**GHF**), **Gifted Education Family Network**, and **PGRetreat.org**.

Zenliving.com

"I suppose the one quality in an astronaut more powerful than any other is curiosity. They have to get some place nobody's ever been." Astronaut John Glenn

About the Authors

Val Wilson, M.Ed
Consultant, School Gifted
Specialist & Adventurer

Val holds a Master's Degree in Curriculum and Instruction and several certifications and endorsements, including gifted learners, elementary education, adult education, reading, English Language Arts, English as a Second Language, and math. Val has been teaching for over three decades and currently works as a gifted specialist and coach for a Title I School. As a teacher leader on her campus, Val leads the MTSS process and supports multiple Professional Learning Communities. She also continues to teach instructional techniques at the college and professional development level online and in person.

In her spare time, Val is the Public Art Commissioner of the City of Youngtown, AZ, who recruits and supports local gifted artists. She is also CEO of Veldazio Rudolpho, her artwork design label and company.

"The energy of the mind is the essence of life."
– Aristotle

The Gifted & Struggling Series

The titles:

*What Parents
Need To Know
2023/24*

*What Educators Need
to Know
2023/24*

*Essential 2e Teaching
Strategies That Are Also
Good For All Learners
2024*

*What School
Administers
Need To Know
2025*

*What School Mental Health Professionals
Need To Know
2025*

Our book series allows for positive collaborations between all stakeholders through a consistent use of conceptual definitions, philosophy, pedagogy, and applications. This allows for a common starting point to understand, communicate, and serve students' needs holistically through robust discussions between stakeholders. What happens at home impacts the school, and the reverse is true.

Main Points of the Series

1. Lead with gifts - your child is gifted first!

2. A twice-exceptional learner always shows an interaction between high abilities (yellow) and complex challenges (blue). Using Susan Baum and colleagues' color metaphor, a 2e child is always green (yellow interacting with blue).

3. The NEST! Perspective is a human development guiding framework to nurture sustainable growth and well-being across our developmental lifespan.

Ask us about our workshops, consulting, professional development, & events!

We love working with groups and ensure that every workshop and event is tailored to the group's needs. Please let us know how we can support you!

You can contact us at:
adam@brightchildbooks.com

Books in our Trauma Support Series

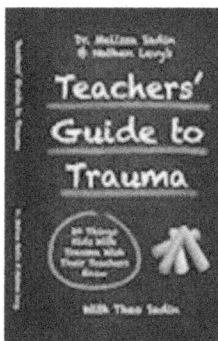

Dr. Melissa Sadin & Nathan Levy's
Teachers' Guide to Trauma
20 Things Kids with Trauma Wish Their Teachers Knew
With Theo Sadin

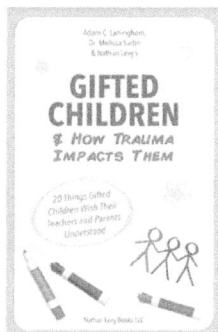

Adam C. Laningham, Dr. Melissa Sadin & Nathan Levy's
GIFTED CHILDREN & HOW TRAUMA IMPACTS THEM
20 Things Gifted Children Wish Their Teachers and Parents Understood
Nathan Levy Books LLC

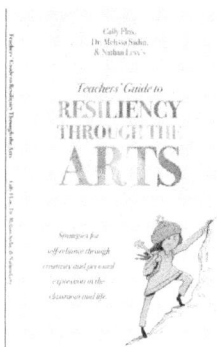

Cally Flox, Dr. Melissa Sadin, & Nathan Levy's
Teachers' Guide to **RESILIENCY THROUGH THE ARTS**
Strategies for effectiveness through creative and personal expression in the classroom and life.

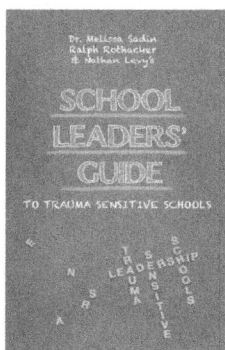

Dr. Melissa Sadin, Ralph Rothacker & Nathan Levy's
SCHOOL LEADERS' GUIDE
TO TRAUMA SENSITIVE SCHOOLS

Made in the USA
Las Vegas, NV
10 May 2024